7.1

BIRDS

BALD EAGLES

James E. Gerholdt
ABDO & Daughters

Published by Abdo & Daughters, 4940 Viking Drive, Suite 622, Edina, Minnesota 55435.

Copyright © 1997 by Abdo Consulting Group, Inc., Pentagon Tower, P.O. Box 36036, Minneapolis, Minnesota 55435 USA. International copyrights reserved in all countries. No part of this book may be reproduced in any form without written permission from the publisher.

Printed in the United States.

Cover and Interior Photo credits: Peter Arnold, Inc.

Edited by Julie Berg

Library of Congress Cataloging-in-Publication Data

Gerholdt, James E., 1943—
       Bald Eagles/James E. Gerholdt.
              p.   cm. -- (birds)
       Includes index.
       Summary: Describes the physical characteristics, habits, and natural habitat of the bird which is our national symbol and which is often used on flags and other official banners.
       ISBN 1-56239-584-X
       1. Bald eagle--Juvenile literature. [1. Bald eagle. 2. Eagles.] I. Title.   II. Series: Gerholdt, James E., 1943—Birds.
       QL696.F32G47   1996
       598.9'16--dc20
                                                                      95-51268
                                                                      CIP
                                                                      AC

Contents

BALD EAGLES

Bald eagles belong to one of the 28 **orders** of **birds**. They are in the same **family** as hawks, and are **raptors**, or birds of prey.

Birds are **vertebrates**. This means they have backbones, just like humans. They are also **warm-blooded**.

Because of **pesticides**, these beautiful birds were once **endangered**. But laws that protect bald eagles and where they live have helped them make a strong comeback.

The bald eagle is the national symbol of America. Its image is often used on flags. A bald eagle in flight is a magnificent sight!

Opposite page: A bald eagle in flight.

SIZES

Bald eagles are large **birds**. The females are larger than the males, and can weigh 10 to 14 pounds (4.5 to 6.4 kg). The males weigh 8 to 9 pounds (3.6 to 4 kg). From the tip of the beak to the tip of the tail, they can measure 34 to 43 inches (86 to 109 cm).

The **wingspan** is 6 to 7 1/2 feet (1.8 to 2.3 m). This broad wingspan is what makes a bald eagle look so large when in flight.

Opposite page: A bald eagle spreading its huge wings, which can span up to 7.5 feet (2.3 m).

SHAPES

The bald eagle is a heavy-bodied **bird**, with long and powerful wings. The head has large eyes and a very large beak. The legs are long and the feet have strong **talons** for grabbing food. The tail is long and wide.

The eagle's **feathers** help it fly and glide while hunting its **prey**. By tilting the wing and tail feathers, the bird can turn and climb through the air.

The wings are kept straight when soaring or gliding. The feet and legs are carried against the belly while the eagle is in flight.

Opposite page: The beak of a bald eagle is large and sharp.

COLORS

Male and female bald eagles have the same colors. Their snow-white heads make them easy to see. The tail is also white.

The body and **feathered** part of the legs are a brownish-black color. The bare part of the legs and the feet are yellow. The eyes and the powerful beak are also yellow.

Young bald eagles are almost all brown. They have some white feathers under the wings, and a brownish beak. They change colors when they are four or five years old.

Opposite page: The bald eagle has a white head, from which it gets its name.

WHERE THEY LIVE

The bald eagle can be found in Alaska, through Canada and the Great Lakes area, and all the way to Florida and Baja California. It can also be found in Siberia and Sweden, and has been seen on the island of Bermuda in the Atlantic Ocean.

These **birds** usually live near oceans, large rivers, or lakes. At times, several dozen can be seen **perched** in fir trees. This happens when eagles **migrate**.

Bald eagles perched in a spruce tree.

SENSES

Bald eagles have the same five senses as humans. Their senses of taste and smell are not very good. But these senses are not very important to them.

Bald eagles rely mostly on their sight. Without this, they could not find food while in flight.

When **prey** is sighted, bald eagles change from long-range vision to near-vision to help them during the hunt. Since their eyes can't turn very far, they must move their heads to see from one side to another.

Eagles have large, powerful eyes.

14

A bald eagle flying toward its prey.

DEFENSE

An adult bald eagle has little to fear from other **birds** or animals. Their keen eyesight, powerful beaks and **talons,** and flying ability protected them against all but one enemy—humans!

Even though they are protected by law, bald eagles are shot and killed. Sometimes they are caught in traps that have been set for other animals. They also might be electrocuted if they land on high-power electrical lines.

Certain **pesticides** were once the main threat to bald eagles. But most of these pesticides are not used anymore.

*A bald eagle battling with another bird
for its fishing territory.*

FOOD

The most important kind of food to a bald eagle is fish. Eagles catch fish with their **talons**. Sometimes they will steal fish from other birds.

Eagles also eat ducks that have been wounded by hunters. Other animals caught for food include muskrats, rabbits, and squirrels.

Another kind of food is **carrion,** which includes animals that have been killed by cars. Sometimes an eagle will eat an animal that has been poisoned and the eagle will die!

Opposite page: A bald eagle feeding on salmon.

BABIES

All bald eagles hatch from eggs. The eggs are large— 2 3/4 by 2 1/8 inches (71 x 54 mm)—and have a rough, white shell. Eggs are often laid two at a time. But sometimes one or three are laid.

The female bald eagle lays her eggs in the largest nests built by any **bird**—often 12 feet (3.7 m) high and 8 1/2 feet (4.25 m) across.

Most nests are built near the tops of tall trees. But some may be on rocky ledges. Their nests are made of sticks and branches, and lined with grass and plants.

The young hatch after 35 to 46 days. They will leave the nest after 10 to 11 weeks.

Opposite page: Baby bald eagles, or "eaglets."

GLOSSARY

bird - A feathered animal with a backbone whose front limbs are wings.

carrion (KAIR-e-on) - Dead and rotting flesh.

endangered - Almost extinct.

family (FAM-uh-lee) - A grouping of animals.

feather (FETH-er) - The light, flat structures covering a bird's body.

migrate (MY-grait) - To move from one place to another.

order (OAR-der) - A grouping of animals.

perch - A bar or branch on which a bird can rest; also, to rest or sit.

pesticide (PESS-tuh-side) - A chemical used to kill pests such as insects.

prey (PRAY) - An animal hunted or seized for food.

raptor (RAP-tore) - A bird that eats other animals.

talons (TAAL-onz) - The claws of a raptor.

vertebrate (VER-tuh-brit) - An animal with a backbone.

warm-blooded - Regulating body temperature at a constant level, from inside the body.

wingspan - The distance from one wing tip to the other.

INDEX